JESUS

COMPASSIONATE HEALER

BILL DONAHUE
& KERI WYATT KENT

IVP Connect

InterVarsity Press
Downers Grove, Illinois

Inter-Varsity Press
Leicester, England

InterVarsity Press, USA
P.O. Box 1400, Downers Grove, IL 60515-1426, USA
World Wide Web: www.ivpress.com
E-mail: mail@ivpress.com

Inter-Varsity Press, England
38 De Montfort Street, Leicester LE1 7GP, England
Website: www.ivpbooks.com
E-mail: ivp@ivp-editorial.co.uk

InterVarsity Press®, USA, is the book-publishing division of InterVarsity Christian Fellowship/USA®, a student movement active on campus at hundreds of universities, colleges and schools of nursing in the United States of America, and a member movement of the International Fellowship of Evangelical Students. For information about local and regional activities, write Public Relations Dept., InterVarsity Christian Fellowship/USA, 6400 Schroeder Rd., P.O. Box 7895, Madison, WI 53707-7895, or visit the IVCF website at <www.intervarsity.org>.

Inter-Varsity Press, England, is the publishing division of the Universities and Colleges Christian Fellowship (formerly the Inter-Varsity Fellowship), a student movement linking Christian Unions in universities and colleges throughout Great Britain, and a member movement of the International Fellowship of Evangelical Students. For information about local and national activities write to UCCF, 38 De Montfort Street, Leicester LE1 7GP, email us at email@uccf.org.uk, or visit the UCCF website at www.uccf.org.uk.

Design: Cindy Kiple
Images: Gary S. & Vivian Chapman/Getty Images

USA ISBNs   0-8308-2156-2
*   978-0-8308-2156-3*

UK ISBNs   1-84474-113-3
*   978-1-84474-113-7*

Printed in the United States of America ∞

P	19	18	17	16	15	14	13	12	11	10	9	8	7	6	5	4	3	2	1
Y	19	18	17	16	15	14	13	12	11	10	09	08	07	06	05				

CONTENTS

Before You Begin 5

INTRODUCTION: JESUS THE COMPASSIONATE HEALER . . 11

   1 Jesus Weeps Our Tears 13

   2 Jesus Binds Our Wounds 19

   3 Jesus Carries Our Burdens 24

   4 Jesus Breaks Our Chains 29

   5 Jesus Covers Our Shame 34

   6 Jesus Restores Our Community 40

Notes for Leaders 45

BEFORE YOU BEGIN

The Jesus 101 series is designed to help you respond to Jesus as you encounter him in the stories and teachings of the Bible, particularly the Gospel accounts of the New Testament. The "101" designation does not mean "simple"; it means "initial." You probably took introductory-level courses in high school or at a university, like Economics 101 or Biology 101. Each was an initial course, a first encounter with the teachings and principles of the subject matter. I had my first encounter with economic theory in Econ 101, but it was not necessarily simple or always easy (at least not for me!).

Jesus 101 may be the first time you looked closely at Jesus. For the first time you will encounter his grace and love, be exposed to his passion and mission, and get a firsthand look at the way he connects with people like you and me. Or perhaps, like me, you have been a Christian many years. In that case you will encounter Jesus for the first time all over again. Often when I read a biblical account of an event in Jesus' life, even if the text is very familiar to me, I am amazed at a new insight or a fresh, personal connection with Jesus I hadn't experienced before.

I believe Jesus 101 will challenge your thinking and stir your soul regardless of how far along the spiritual pathway you might be. After all, Jesus is anything but dull: he tended to shake up the world of everyone who interacted with him. Sometimes people sought him out; often he surprised them. In every case, he challenged them, evoking a reaction they could hardly ignore.

There are many ways we might encounter Jesus. In this series we will focus on eight. You will come face to face with Jesus as

- Provocative Teacher
- Sacred Friend
- Extreme Forgiver
- Authentic Leader
- Truthful Revealer
- Compassionate Healer
- Relentless Lover
- Supreme Conqueror

☐ HOW THESE GUIDES ARE PUT TOGETHER

In each of the discussion guides you will find material for six group meetings, though feel free to use as many meetings as necessary to cover the material. That is up to you. Each group will find its way. The important thing is to encounter and connect with Christ, listen to what he is saying, watch what he is doing—and then personalize that encounter individually and as a group.

The material is designed to help you engage with one another, with the Bible and with the person of Jesus. The experiences below are designed to guide you along when you come together as a group.

Gathering to Listen

This short section orients you to the material by using an illustration, a quote or a text that raises probing questions, makes provocative assumptions or statements, or evokes interpersonal tension or thoughtfulness. It may just make you laugh. It sets the tone for the dialogue you will be having together. Take a moment here to connect with one another and focus your attention on the reading. Listen carefully as thoughts and emotions are stirred.

After the reading, you will have an opportunity to respond in some way. What are your first impressions, your assumptions, disagreements, feelings? What comes to mind as you read this?

Encountering Jesus

Here you meet Jesus as he is described in the Bible text. You will encounter his teachings, his personal style and his encounters with people much like you. This section will invite your observations, questions and initial reactions to what Jesus is saying and doing.

Joining the Conversation

A series of group questions and interactions will encourage your little community to engage with one another about the person and story of Jesus. Here you will remain for a few moments in the company of Jesus and of one another. This section may pose a question about your group or ask you to engage in an exercise or interaction with one another. The goal is to discover a sense of community as you question and discover what God is doing.

Connecting Our Stories

Here you are invited to connect your story (life, issues, questions, challenges) with Jesus' story (his teaching, character and actions). We look at our background and history, the things that encourage or disappoint us. We seek to discover what God is doing in our life and the lives of others, and we develop a sense of belonging and understanding.

Finding Our Way

A final section of comments and questions invites you to investigate next steps for your spiritual journey as a group and personally. It will evoke and prompt further action, decisions or conversations in response to what was discovered and discussed. You will prompt one another to listen to God more deeply, take relational risks and invite God's work in your group and in the community around you.

Praying Together

God's Holy Spirit is eager to teach you! Remember that learning is not just a mental activity; it involves relationship and action. One educator suggests that all learning is the result of failed expectations. We hope, then, that at some point your own expectations will fail, that you will be ambushed by the truth and stumble into new and unfamiliar territory that startles you into new ways of thinking about God and relating to him through Christ. And so prayer—talking and listening to God—is a vital part of the Jesus 101 journey.

If you are seeking to discover Jesus for the first time, your prayer can be a very simple expression of your thoughts and questions to God. It may include emotions like anger, frustration, joy or wonder. If you already have an intimate, conversational relationship with God, your prayer will reflect the deepest longings and desires of your soul. Prayer is an integral part of the spiritual life, and small groups are a great place to explore it.

☐ HOW DO I PREPARE?

No preparation is required! Reading the Bible text ahead of time, if you can, will provide an overview of what lies ahead and will give you an opportunity to reflect on the Bible passages. But you will not feel out of the loop or penalized in some way if you do not get to it. This material is designed for *group* discovery and interaction. A sense of team and community develops and excitement grows as you explore the material together. In contrast to merely discussing what everyone has already discovered prior to the meeting, "discovery in the moment" evokes a sense of shared adventure.

If you want homework, do that after each session. Decide how you might face your week, your job, your relationships and family in light of what you have just discovered about Jesus.

☐ A FINAL NOTE

These studies are based on the book *In the Company of Jesus*. It is not required that you read the book to do any Jesus 101 study—each stands alone. But you might consider reading the parallel sections of the book to enrich your experience between small group meetings. The major sections of the book take up the same eight ways that we encounter Jesus in the Jesus 101 guides. So the eight guides mirror the book in structure and themes, but the material in the book is not identical to that of the guides.

Jesus 101 probes more deeply into the subject matter, whereas *In the Company of Jesus* is designed for devotional and contemplative reading and prayer. It is filled with stories and anecdotes to inspire and motivate you in your relationship with Christ.

I pray and hope that you enjoy this adventure as you draw truth from the Word of God for personal transformation, group growth and living out God's purposes in the world!

INTRODUCTION

THE COMPASSIONATE HEALER

December 26, 2004, will live in infamy for the millions who reside in coastline areas devastated by the tsunami that struck after an earthquake below the Indian Ocean. Indonesia and Sri Lanka felt the brunt of the tidal wave, which traveled as far as the African coast, and the death toll was probably over 240,000, with disease killing thousands more in the aftermath.

The scope of the disaster was rivaled only by the outpouring of compassion from around the world. In the ensuing days, over $4 billion in relief was pledged by the global community. Relief organizations, governments, churches, businesses, schools and individuals of every color and creed sought to respond with medical supplies, food, water and housing.

The expressions of compassion were not limited to adults and established organizations. Young people around the world gave to the cause. In America we were moved as we heard the stories. "Kids in Michigan sold hot chocolate; in North Carolina they sold lemonade; students in an 8th-grade class in Wenatchee, Washington, voted unanimously to give their class trip money, which they had been raising for more than a year, to the Red Cross" (Nancy Gibbs, "Race Against Time," *Time,* January 17, 2005).

When hearts are truly stirred by the suffering and pain of others, the outpouring of love and hope is hard to measure. More than almost anything else, acts of compassion have the potential to heal physical and emotional wounds, restore relationships, dispel hatred and curb violence. The power of compassion is one of the most underrated forces on the planet.

No one person embodied God's heart of compassion for people in distress more than Jesus of Nazareth. His heart broke for the sick, the poor, the hungry, the outcast and the weary. And his heart is moved toward you and me as well. In our pain and grief, our confusion and suffering, Jesus meets us with healing grace and love. When it feels as if we have been struck by a physical, relational or financial tsunami that crushes our spirit and robs our hope, the compassion of Jesus Christ is available and flows freely.

ONE

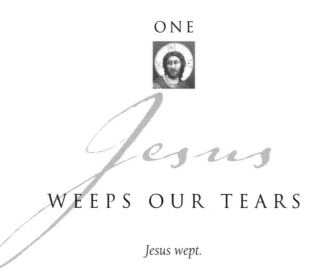

Jesus WEEPS OUR TEARS

Jesus wept.

☐ **GATHERING TO LISTEN**

In his book *Windows of the Soul,* Ken Gire observes:

> Perhaps there are no greater windows of the soul than our tears.
>
> The tears we cry are drawn from the well of who we are, a well that lies beneath the sedimentary strata of words, beneath even the Pre-cambrian layer of consciousness itself. They may seep to the surface like the smallest of subterranean springs or shoot to the surface like a geyser. They surface for odd reasons, or for no reason at all, or for reasons so pure and right and good that no force on earth could hold them back. . . .
>
> So much is distilled in our tears, not the least of which is wisdom in living life. From my own tears I have learned that if you follow your tears, you will find your heart. If you find your heart, you will find what is dear to God. And if you find what is dear to God, you will find the answer to how you should live your life.

- What is your response to Gire's thoughts?
- What have your own tears taught you?

☐ ENCOUNTERING JESUS

In this passage we see Jesus's response to the tears of his friends.

Read John 11:1-37.

1. Jesus heard about Lazarus's life-threatening illness but didn't go to see him for two days. Do you find this unusual?

2. The disciples of Jesus are fearful of his return to Judea because of a death threat. He goes nonetheless because he has a greater purpose than self-preservation. How do the disciples respond, and what is their attitude (verses 11-16)?

3. What do you notice about the things Mary and Martha say to Jesus?

   What is their attitude when he first arrives, and how does that change?

WHY DID JESUS WAIT?

Many often wonder why Jesus waited to travel to Bethany from the Perean countryside across the Jordan. After all, he responded immediately to the widow in Nain whose son had died (Luke 7:11-16) and to Jairus's request to heal his daughter (Luke 8:41-56). Why wait now? Why take so long? Verses 4-5, 11-14 provide some of the reasons.

Jesus' waiting should not be interpreted as a lack of compassion, though on the surface it certainly is difficult to understand. God's glory is always more important than our satisfaction or pleasure. Jesus had a greater mission, and the death, not healing, of Lazarus was central to his mission. Lazarus's resurrection was a foreshadowing of Jesus' resurrection, and it drove religious leaders to plan to get rid of Jesus (11:45-57).

Jesus also wanted to teach his followers about hope in the resurrection. This hope was to be centered in who he was—the Christ, the Son of God—and in what he was about to do (raise Lazarus as a demonstration of his power to raise the dead). Verses 40-42 give us an even greater purpose for this raising of Lazarus. Jesus wanted to demonstrate that belief in him would allow people to see God's power and glory.

4. Consider Jesus' response to Mary and Martha, especially the tears of
   Mary. Though he knows he is about to raise Lazarus from the dead,
   he weeps and is moved deeply. What does this tell you about Jesus?
   (See especially verses 33-36.)

□ JOINING THE CONVERSATION

5. Reflect on how you respond to the suffering and death of people you
   know and love. What do you find disturbing or encouraging about
   Jesus' response here?

6. Based on this story of Jesus, what words would you use to describe
   him?

   Would any of these words also be used to describe you?

□ CONNECTING OUR STORIES

7. American funerals are often brief, followed by a meal. But in other
   cultures it is normal to mourn together for days, as we see in this

story. What has been your experience of dealing with grief and sorrow?

Have you ever had someone mourn with you over a death or difficulty in your life? If so, talk about that experience.

8. Each of us has shed tears of grief or sorrow. Does it make a difference to know that Jesus shares in that sorrow, embraces our tears and offers comfort? Or do you feel God does not care about your pain?

9. What does the resurrection of Lazarus mean for those of us who weep and mourn?

☐ **FINDING OUR WAY**

10. Verses 25-27 are some of the most powerful in the Bible. Having a clear picture of who Jesus is will affect how we view life, friendship, suffering and death. Has your view of Jesus changed by reading this story?

How might that play out in your life?

11. There is comfort now and resurrection hope for the future for all who mourn. Take a moment to express your grief and hope to each other. You may want to express your emotions to God and others in a journal or on a notepad, and then share some of these in groups of two or three.

☐ PRAYING TOGETHER

Remaining in small groups of two or three, spend some time in quietness. Read Psalm 6 and reflect on a time when you felt sadness, even shed tears. Were you aware of God's presence with you at that time? If not, ask him to meet you now as you remember that situation. Ask him to bring comfort and hope. The power and love of Christ is available now—directly and through the embrace and prayers of others in the group.

Spend some time praying as a group, thanking Jesus for embracing each of us in our tears, whether they were tears of sadness, disappointment, loneliness or grief.

TWO

Jesus
BINDS OUR WOUNDS

He had compassion on them and healed their sick.

☐ **GATHERING TO LISTEN**

In *Waking the Dead,* John Eldredge writes about the wounds of our hearts and how God wants to restore our hearts so that we can be "fully alive."

> Walking with God leads to receiving his intimate counsel, and counseling leads to deep restoration. As we learn to walk with God and hear his voice, he is able to bring up issues in our hearts that need speaking to. Some of those wounds were enough to break our hearts, create a rift in the soul, and so we need his healing as well. This is something Jesus walks us into—sometimes through the help of another person who can listen and pray with us, sometimes with God alone. As David said in Psalm 23, he leads us away, to a quiet place, to restore the soul. Our first choice is to go with him there—to slow down, unplug, accept the invitation to come aside.

> If we were physically wounded, it would be extremely difficult for a doctor or anyone else to treat and bandage our wounds if we kept run-

ning around. Often, though, we try to ignore the wounds in our heart by keeping ourselves running, moving fast. We are afraid to slow down, but our sitting still will give Jesus the opportunity to care for us.

• How do you respond to Eldredge's statement?

☐ ENCOUNTERING JESUS

Read Mark 5:21-43.

The woman in the story has been suffering with reproductive health issues for twelve years. In our day, this would be bad enough. But in Jewish society at that time, a woman in this condition would be considered "unclean" and would have to announce that out loud everywhere she went. Imagine the pain of this woman: not only an ongoing health issue, not only distress about how doctors had taken her money and left her worse off than before, but also the shame of having to declare herself unclean and of being shunned by others everywhere she went.

1. The woman has seen many doctors and spent all her money. How do you think she feels about her life?

Why do you think she comes up and secretly touches Jesus?

2. Jesus feels her touch and stops to ask who touched him. Why do you think Jesus does this? (Doesn't he know all things?)

3. What does this account teach us about how the power of Jesus?

4. Jesus tells the woman, "Your faith has healed you." But according to the story, it is touching Jesus that heals the woman. Which is it, or is it both?

□ JOINING THE CONVERSATION

5. The disciples, eager to get Jesus to Jairus's daughter, who is dying, seem annoyed by Jesus' question and unaware of what is happening. What does their response to Jesus tell you about them?

6. The afflicted woman has the faith to touch Jesus yet is trembling with fear. Do you ever find yourself in a similar position with God, interested in getting closer to him but afraid of what might happen as a result?

7. If Jesus had just let the woman go without saying anything, she still would have been healed. What wound does Jesus heal by speaking to her?

☐ **CONNECTING OUR STORIES**

8. The woman in the story is so desperate for healing that she disobeys her culture's prohibition of an unclean person's touching a rabbi. Have you ever been so desperate for healing that you took desperate measures? Describe the situation.

9. What are your thoughts about the connection between our faith and Jesus' power to heal our wounds?

What similarities and/or differences do you see between your story and the woman's?

☐ FINDING OUR WAY

10. Where does your group need the healing power of Jesus?

How can you encourage each other to exercise the faith necessary to trust him for that power?

☐ PRAYING TOGETHER

All of us are wounded in some way. Perhaps we have been hurt emotionally or relationally. Perhaps we suffer physical symptoms. Often emotional wounds are the ones we hide, hoping that we can get them healed without having to bring them out in the open.

Spend some time praying that God would give each person in the group the healing they need and the courage to bring those wounds out into the open to let Jesus heal them.

THREE

Jesus

CARRIES OUR BURDENS

*Come to me, all you who are weary and burdened,
and I will give you rest.*

☐ GATHERING TO LISTEN

We all have concerns, challenges and difficulties. We carry burdens,
whether worry, guilt or difficult circumstances. Reflect on your past experience with burdens. Here are some possible situations to prompt
your thinking.

A good report arrived from a doctor.

Your exam—the one you forgot to study for—was postponed by the teacher.

You lost your two-year-old child at the mall, then suddenly found her.

The graduate school you applied to accepted you.

You finally got that cast off your arm or leg after six weeks.

You took your first steps after the serious accident.

Your father became a Christ-follower just months before he died.

A two-year project was finally completed, and the client loved your work.

- What was it like to have a heavy load lifted?

- Now look at the present. Is there a struggle or burden you can briefly tell the group about? Start with a sentence or two that states what you are facing. "My burden is . . ." Spend a few minutes listening to each other, asking God to make you tender to the burdens of others.

- Next, read Isaiah 41:9-14. In this passage God promises to help his people, to strengthen them. How does God help us?

☐ **ENCOUNTERING JESUS**

Hearing these promises in Isaiah begins to lighten the burdens we carry. Now let us consider what it would be like to give Jesus our burdens.

Read Luke 11:46, then Matthew 9:35-38.

1. Jesus' comment to the religious leaders in Luke 11:46 is just part of a scathing critique of the Pharisees and their lifestyle of hypocrisy. How do these "experts in the law" place burdens on people?

In Jesus' day, Pharisees were extremely zealous about their religious traditions and sought to rigorously practice the Torah, the five books of Moses, the Law. Most of their influence was in and around Jerusalem where the Jewish temple was the center of religious life. Repeatedly the Pharisees challenged Jesus to authenticate his credentials as a rabbi. As Jesus' popularity grows, they feel threatened and ultimately conspire with other to plot his death.

---

2. Why is Jesus so concerned with their misinterpretation of the law?

3. The Pharisees had much influence on people's spiritual condition. How might they have made people feel "harassed and helpless"?

4. Jesus preaches "the good news." What do you think his original hearers found so good about it?

☐ JOINING THE CONVERSATION

5. Jesus saw that people around him were lost, "like sheep without a shepherd." His response, the text says, was compassion. What does that response tell you about Jesus as a person?

Is it what you expected from Jesus?

6. When you encounter people who are wandering away from God, or frazzled and helpless, how do you typically respond?

☐ CONNECTING OUR STORIES

7. Tell of a time when you felt burdened spiritually. Perhaps your church's teachings were unreasonably demanding, or a person "loaded you up with burdens" that you could not carry, or you tried to meet someone's expectations for what a "good Christian" should look like.

8. When you have a heavy burden to carry, what do you do with it?
   • try to deal with it myself
   • hope it goes away
   • share it with others only when my efforts have failed
   • pray and ask God to take it from me
   • try to give it to others and ignore my responsibility
   • ask a close friend to help me carry it
   • connect with my community and ask for help

   Why do you respond this way?

☐ FINDING OUR WAY

9. The "harvest" around us is plentiful. What opportunities to reach out and serve others lie within our grasp?

10. We can be in the "burden loading" or "burden lifting" business. Within your group, how can you be burden lifters for one another? (Briefly read Matthew 11:28-30 and Galatians 6:1-5 for encouragement on what do to with burdens.)

☐ **PRAYING TOGETHER**

The ultimate burden that Jesus carried for us was the burden of our sin. But sometimes the smaller burdens we carry can become our main focus. Spend some time praying for those who are carrying heavy burdens.

Jesus became our sin-bearer. His sacrificial death on the cross was necessary to atone for the sin of all humans. Thus his death satisfied the need for justice, righting the wrong we have all done against a holy and loving God. In his great love for people, God gave us his own Son to be the object of his wrath so that we would not have to bear the guilt of our offenses. Jesus willingly did this, motivated by love and desirous of creating an eternal community of all who love God, follow him and trust in his saving grace. See Romans 3:21-26; Galatians 3:13; and 1 Peter 2:24. For more on this, see the IVP Bible Dictionary *(Downers Grove, Ill.: InterVarsity Press, 1996), pp. 102-4.*

FOUR

BREAKS OUR CHAINS

He has sent me to proclaim freedom for the prisoners.

☐ GATHERING TO LISTEN

Nelson Mandela was unjustly imprisoned for twenty-seven years on Robben Island, across from Cape Town, South Africa. My family had an opportunity to see his cell and to hear the story of his many days of isolation and torment. It is difficult to imagine being held captive for so long, especially under a justice system controlled by people who are seeking to silence you and destroy what you believe in.

Remarkably, Mandela emerged a stronger man. But he had lost many years of his life. He had not been able to eat dinner with friends, watch his children grow up, walk the streets of his favorite towns, or enjoy the beauty of the South African bush and countryside. He was a prisoner in his own country.

When freed, Mandela organized no overthrow of the government; neither did he encourage or entertain the revenge that many of his people advocated. No: now he was free, and his chains were broken. Now was the time for restructuring, healing, forgiveness and progress.

Violence would accomplish none of that.

- Freedom! Fresh air, sunshine, the ability to come and go as one pleases, to choose food and drink, to speak one's heart, to hug one's children. These are the joys and privileges of physical freedom. Yet there are other ways to be in prison and other kinds of freedom. What are some ways that we can be imprisoned?

- What does it mean to be free?

☐ **ENCOUNTERING JESUS**

Sometimes we are bound and chained by physical injuries, limitations or pain. Sometimes we are crippled by legalistic thinking, and our faith is tangled in a web of rules. Jesus came to break all chains that keep us from living a joyful life in relationship with him.

Read Luke 13:10-17.

1. What sorts of "chains" hinder the woman who comes to Jesus in the synagogue?

2. Jesus interrupts his own teaching to call the woman out of the crowd, knowing how the religious leaders will respond. Why do you think he chooses to do it anyway?

3. Here, as in Luke 6:6-11, the religious leaders are furious that Jesus is healing on the sabbath. Based on what you've learned so far about

what the religious leaders of Jesus' day valued, why do you think they are so angry?

☐ **Joining the Conversation**

4. The text says this woman has suffered for eighteen years—perhaps since childhood. Imagine having a physical challenge that would not allow you to stand upright for eighteen years. How would you feel about yourself, about God and about others?

5. Look at Jesus' interaction with each of the following characters mentioned in the story. Based on what the story says, and with a little imagination, tell briefly how each one responds to Jesus.

   • the crippled woman
   • the spirit that has kept her bound
   • the synagogue ruler
   • the people who are watching
   • other religious leaders
   • Satan

Finally, consider your response to Jesus. Place yourself in the story. What do you see, feel and think?

6. The woman is physically bent over. What symbolism do you see in her infirmity and how she responds to her healing?

☐ **CONNECTING OUR STORIES**

7. Ever felt like you were in chains, in bondage—or that you are now? Take a moment to tell someone in the group what that was (is) like.

8. Notice Jesus' words to the woman: "You are set free." Have you ever felt like you have been set free? What were you set free from? Here is a list to prompt your thinking.
   • an addiction or destructive habit
   • an illness or disease
   • an attitude of pride or judgment
   • an oppressive work situation
   • a pejorative view of yourself
   • an abusive relationship
   • an oppressive religious system

☐ **FINDING OUR WAY**

9. The text says that Jesus' "opponents were humiliated" and yet "the people were delighted" at all Jesus was doing. How was Jesus perhaps trying to break the chains that the religious leaders had put on the people?

   How can we allow him to break our chains?

10. How can your group be agents of grace and change, to help each other find freedom and break the chains that keep you from standing tall and praising God?

☐ **PRAYING TOGETHER**

Jesus said, "You will know the truth, and the truth will set you free." Pray that each person in the group would know truth and that it would break the chains that hold them back from giving glory to God with words, with their actions, with their life.

FIVE

COVERS OUR SHAME

Your sins are forgiven.

☐ GATHERING TO LISTEN

In Nathaniel Hawthorne's classic story *The Scarlet Letter*, the main character is a woman who has been caught in adultery. As a result of her sin in the community, she is forced to wear a bright red capital *A* on her clothing, exposing her shame for all to see. In this Puritan community she is ostracized and neglected. Her accusers, though they too are filled with sin, are required to wear no such letter. Outwardly they appear innocent, but inwardly they are riddled with pride and self-righteousness. The story examines hidden and exposed sin and the effects of shame.

Often we feel that people have labeled us, that we are wearing a scarlet letter of shame. Our sin feels overwhelming enough to destroy us. But God says, "Though your sins be as scarlet, they will be as white as snow" (Isaiah 1:18).

God has a remedy for shame, and it is found in the person of Jesus of Nazareth.

- Tell about a time growing up when you felt as if you, like Hawthorne's character, were wearing a pejorative label on your clothing. Perhaps it was a word like *coward,* or *ugly,* or *liar,* or *loser,* or *unworthy.* What did it feel like?
- How did it affect your understanding of yourself?

☐ **ENCOUNTERING JESUS**

Read John 8:1-11.

1. Jesus is teaching early in the morning at the temple, and a lot of people have gathered around him. How do you imagine the Pharisees are feeling about Jesus' popularity as a teacher?

2. Jesus often taught by saying, "You have heard it said . . . but I say . . ." The Pharisees turn this around on him here and cite the Jewish law as reason for them to kill the woman caught in adultery. The text says they are trying to trap Jesus. What do you think they are trying to trap him into doing?

3. Jesus doesn't answer right away. What does he do instead of answering?

Why do you think he does this?

4. What does Jesus' response to the woman and her accusers tell you about him?

☐ JOINING THE CONVERSATION

5. Read the quote on page 37 by Michael Card. What do you think about Card's observations? Do you agree or disagree? Why?

6. Working in twos or threes, define the following terms:
   • accusation
   • judgment
   • condemnation

   Based on what you understand about these terms, discuss what is happening in the story.

It was what he did not say that spoke most powerfully to the mob that morning. It was a cup of cold water for a thirsty adulteress and an ice-cold drenching in the face to a group of angry Pharisees.

To this day we have not the slightest idea what it was Jesus twice scribbled in the sand. By and large the commentaries have asked the wrong question through the ages. They labor over content, over what he might have written. They ask what without ever realizing that the real question is why. It was not the content that mattered, but why he did it. Unexpected. Irritating. Creative. . . .

What Jesus did that morning created a space in time that allowed the angry mob first to cool down, then to hear his word, and finally to think about it, be convicted by it and respond—or not. . . . It was a response to the noise and confusion and busyness all around him, yet it was not in the least tainted by the noise. Instead, Jesus' action created a frame around the silence—the kind of silence in which God speaks to the heart. In short, it was a supreme act of creativity. It was art.

MICHAEL CARD, *Scribbling in the Sand*

☐ **CONNECTING OUR STORIES**

7. Have you ever been caught in the act of doing something you knew was wrong? Or have you ever been falsely accused but powerless to refute the claim? What was it like?

8. How do you imagine that this woman feels after hearing the words of Jesus?

☐ **FINDING OUR WAY**

9. What do you notice about the way Jesus responds to the woman once her accusers have left?

   Why do you suppose he doesn't ask about the details or try to get her side of the story?

10. There is an interesting paradox in Jesus' final words to the woman. He says he does not condemn her, but he does tell her she must change her life, must leave the life of sin she's leading. How can your

group follow Jesus' example when you are interacting with one another?

☐ **PRAYING TOGETHER**

Romans 8:1 says: "Therefore, there is now no condemnation for those who are in Christ Jesus, because through Christ Jesus the law of the Spirit of life set me free from the power of sin and death."

Jesus has covered our shame, and we are no longer condemned. Spend some time thanking him for the freedom that is available through him.

SIX

RESTORES OUR COMMUNITY

. . . That they might be one as we [Jesus and the Father] are one.

☐ **GATHERING TO LISTEN**

Have you ever been on a team that did not function like one? It is very frustrating. You may have all the talent in the world, but if your group is composed only of self-consumed prima donnas whose chief aim is to "watch out for number one," then you do not have a team.

In some activities, individuals may fail but the "team" can still be successful. Tennis teams, track teams and gymnastics teams are collections of individuals who have the same goal—to win. But each member does not depend on the others to perform well. These "teams" are mostly built on solo performances.

Members of other teams—like orchestras, soccer teams and firefighters—depend on one another to get the job done right. If one or two persons fail, the whole team may collapse. On a track team, if the high jumper loses her event, the team's score could still be high enough for it to win the event. But imagine the soccer goalie having a terrible game, or the cello player lagging one measure behind the rest of the string quartet, or the driver of a fire truck making a wrong turn. In each of these cases, if one fails, the whole team suffers. Everyone is needed, and they all must work together to achieve the desired result.

- Tell about a time you had to work closely as a team or a group. What happened when someone did not show up or performed poorly?

- Now read Psalm 133 and reflect on what the psalmist says. What comes about as the result of unity?

☐ ENCOUNTERING JESUS

In order for the community of God's people to function well, we are all needed. Jesus Christ came to unite us in community because everything in the kingdom is better when it is done together, whether it be prayer, worship, study, serving the poor or sharing the message of God's love for the world. Ephesians 4:16 says, "From [Christ] the whole body, joined and held together by every supporting ligament, grows and builds itself up in love, *as each part does its work.*" We are all needed as part of the community, and it works better when we come together.

Read John 17:6-26.

Jesus has been talking with his disciples, telling them about the trials he is about to endure and teaching them what it means to follow him. Now Jesus is praying for his disciples, and for the believers who will hear Jesus' message through his followers. One of the central themes of this prayer is oneness, an essential unity that should characterize Jesus' followers.

1. In verses 6-10 Jesus describes his relationship with his closest followers. What are some of the characteristics of this relationship?

2. What do you think Jesus means when he asks God the Father to protect his followers "so that they may be one as we are one" (verse 11)?

3. Jesus prays this prayer out loud for his disciples. What does he hope will happen as a result of praying for them?

4. Look at verses 13-19. Jesus mentions the kinds of things he wants to see in the community he has just begun. List some characteristics of this new community.

☐ JOINING THE CONVERSATION

5. Jesus is very concerned about oneness and unity. Based on verses 20-23, why is this so important to him?

6. Jesus prays that "all of them may be one, Father, just as you are in me and I am in you. May they also be in us." What does he mean by this?

What does it teach us about his relationships?

7. All over the world, wars are fought over religious differences. Within Christianity, there are numerous theologies, denominations and doctrines. There are many issues well-meaning Christians disagree about. Does this mean that Jesus' prayer will go unanswered? Do you think the unity that he prayed for will ever actually come about? Why or why not?

☐ **CONNECTING OUR STORIES**

8. What does it takes to live in complete unity with someone? List some of the key factors.

9. Read Ephesians 4:1-5. According to this passage, what attitudes will help promote unity?

What do we need to do to help make Jesus' vision of unity a reality?

10. Our unity is not just for our sake. Jesus prays for our unity because it will demonstrate love to the world. How might the outside world view the church if we allowed a spirit of unity to develop among us?

☐ **FINDING OUR WAY**

11. Action steps: Discuss how, as members of a small group community, you need one another. How can you connect with one another more deeply over the coming week?

☐ **PRAYING TOGETHER**

Jesus desires our unity in love, truth and commitment to his cause of world redemption. Pray that you can work together to promote that kind of unity. And pray for one another as you face conflict and division in relationships, marriage, family life and work. Pray that all in the group and those connected to people in the group would allow walls of division to be removed and that they would live together in unity.

NOTES FOR LEADERS

Each session has a similar format using the components below. Here is a very rough guide for the amount of time you might spend on each segment for a ninety-minute meeting time, excluding additional social time. This is a general guide, and you will learn to adjust the format as you become comfortable working together as a group:

Gathering to Listen	5-10 minutes
Encountering Jesus	15 minutes
Joining the Conversation	20 minutes
Connecting Our Stories	20 minutes
Finding Our Way	10 minutes
Praying Together	about 10 minutes

You can take some shortcuts or take longer as the group decides, but strive to stay on schedule for a ninety-minute meeting including prayer time. You will also want to save time to attend to personal needs and prayer. This will vary by group and can also be accomplished in personal relationships you develop between meetings.

As group leader, know that you help create an environment for spiritual growth. Here are a few things to consider as you invite people to follow in the company of Jesus.

LEADER TIPS

Practice authenticity and truth telling. Do not pretend an elephant is not sitting in the middle of the room when everyone knows it is.

- Does your group have a commitment to pursue personal change and growth?
- Set some ground rules or a covenant for group interactions. Consider values like confidentiality, respect and integrity.
- Model and encourage healthy self-disclosure through icebreakers, storytelling and getting to know one another between meetings.

CONNECTING SEEKERS TO JESUS

This simple process is designed to help you guide a person toward commitment to Christ. It is only a guide, intended to give you the feel of a conversation you might have.

1. *Describe what you see going on.* "Mike, I sense you are open to knowing Jesus more personally. Is this the case?"

2. *Affirm that Jesus is always inviting people to follow him (John 6:35-40).* "Mike, Jesus has opened the door to a full and dynamic relationship with him. All who believe in Jesus are welcome. Do you want to place your trust in Jesus?"

3. *Describe how sin has separated us from God, making a relationship with God impossible (Romans 3:21-26).* "Though Jesus desires fellowship with us, our sin stands in the way. So Jesus went to the cross to pay for that sin, to take away the guilt of that sin and to make reconciliation with God possible again. Are you aware that your sin has become a barrier between you and Jesus?"

4. *Show how Jesus' death on the cross bridged the gap between us and God (Romans 5:1-11).* "Now we can have peace with God, a relationship with Jesus, because his death canceled out our sin debt. All our offenses against God are taken away by Jesus."

5. *Invite them to have a brief conversation with God (2 Corinthians 5:11—6:2).* "By asking for his forgiveness and being reconnected to Jesus, we can have new life, one that starts now. Jesus invites you to join him in this new life—to love him, learn his ways, connect to his people and trust in his purposes. We can talk to him now and express that desire if you want to."

These five suggestions are designed to create a dialogue and discern if a person wants to follow Jesus. Points to remember:

1. Keep it authentic and conversational.
2. God is at work here—you are simply a guide, leading someone toward a step of faith in Jesus.
3. The heart is more important than the specific words.
4. People will not understand all that Christ has done, so don't try to confuse them with too much information.
5. Keep it simple.
6. Don't put words in someone's mouth. Let them describe how they want to follow Jesus and participate in his life.

7. Use Scripture as needed. You may recite some or let them read the passages.
8. Remember, this is not a decision to join an organization. It is a relationship with a person, an invitation to a new life and a new community: "Come follow me."

As the person expresses the desire to follow Jesus, encourage them to read the Gospel of Mark and discover the life of Jesus and his teachings more clearly.

SESSION 1.
JESUS WEEPS OUR TEARS.
John 11:1-37.

Gathering to Listen (about 10 minutes). Many of us don't want to open the "windows of the soul"—we'd rather keep them shut up tight. Yet meaningful relationships require us to allow others to see the truth about us. This may be a stretch for some group members. Some people, especially men, have grown up hearing that crying or sadness is wrong. Vulnerability is not something you can demand, especially not from those who are uncomfortable with even the idea of tears. But you can try to make the group a place where it is safe to express a wide range of thoughts, feelings and emotions.

Encountering Jesus (15 minutes). In biblical times deaths were accompanied by great wailing as a community grieved together. Before Jesus raised Jairus's daughter, there was great crying and wailing (Mark 5:38). Burial took place quickly because of the heat and likelihood of decomposition. Caves were used, with shelves for bodies carved into the walls. Each dead body was washed, covered with spices blended into a paste, and wrapped in a linen cloth. In some cases, as here, the head, hands and feet were wrapped tightly with bandages. There were not many caves, so after decomposition the bones were removed and placed in jars called ossuaries. Thus, if a family moved to another town, they could take the bones of relatives with them.

Burial caves were painted white to alert others there were dead people inside, because an Israelite who came into contact with the dead would become ritually unclean (see Exodus 13:19; Leviticus 11:31; 21:11; Matthew 23:27). This may explain why people did not rush to touch Lazarus when he exited the tomb.

They were not only in shock, they had been taught all their lives to avoid unnecessary contact with dead bodies.

Israelites were not all certain of the resurrection (though Daniel 12:2 introduces the concept and Martha affirms this in John 11:24). Pharisees believed in it, while Sadducees did not. Jesus is about to make it very clear to people that there is a resurrection and the power to achieve it lies in belief in him.

Joining the Conversation (20 minutes). Mostly Jesus' sadness shows us that he was fully human as well as divine; he really understands our sadness and our tears and disappointments—though we are focused on Jesus' compassion here, this text also reveals aspects of his anger. The language used here portrays Jesus as having a deep, visceral response accompanied by snorting, almost like a horse. He is angry—angry at the effects of sin and the reality of death. His heart is "deeply moved" as he experiences all of the emotions we would feel at the loss of a friend: sorrow, anger and grief.

He is tender, compassionate, loving. But initially he appeared uncaring. Help members understand that God is mysterious (Isaiah 55:8-9) and his purposes often are deeper than ours.

Allow group members to speak honestly, and encourage them to see the full scope of Jesus' emotions and character. He is powerful over death, loving, compassionate, sensitive, obedient to the will of God, all knowing and wise. He tests the faith of Mary and Martha, desiring their spiritual growth, not merely their happiness.

Connecting Our Stories (20 minutes). Shared sadness unites us with other people: when we have been through something difficult together, we experience a special bond. Jesus has shared our sadness. This connected him with Martha and Mary, and also connects him with us, at a deep level.

The purpose of this story is not to teach us about grieving. It is to show us the power of God and is there to strengthen our faith and give us hope in the resurrection from the dead. But it does show us how Jesus responds to those who are grieving. He mourns with those who mourn and is free to express sadness at the death of a close friend.

It has been said that real community begins at the edge of suffering. Shared grief and suffering unite us in ways that prosperity and health do not. The human condition involves brokenness and weakness. We find the strength of God made perfect in our weakness. Paul said, "I want to know Christ and the power of his resurrection and the fellowship of his sufferings, becoming like him in his death, and so, somehow, to attain to the resurrection from the dead" (Philippians 3:10-11).

Be aware that some have not grieved the death of loved ones and may experience some emotion at this point. Be prepared to respond with affection, understanding, your presence and prayer. It is not the group's job to fix people. Allow them to express emotions, thoughts and disappointments as need be. The resurrection of Lazarus is a testimony to all who weep and mourn that God is present and compassionate.

Finding Our Way (10 minutes). We can be vulnerable with Jesus; indeed, Jesus' humanity meant that he too was vulnerable. He really experienced humanity and what it is like to feel pain and sadness. Sometimes it is hard for us to be honest with Jesus, but this passage shows us that he knows what it is like to be human. He has experienced not only the events of a human life but also the emotions that go with them.

Praying Together (about 10 minutes). Don't hurry through this exercise. It may take a bit of time for people to remember pain or grief from the past. Be patient.

SESSION 2.
JESUS BINDS OUR WOUNDS.
Mark 5:21-43.

Gathering to Listen (about 10 minutes). Even if we seem like we've got it all together, each of us is wounded in some way. Each has pain and needs healing. Eldredge argues that it is our heart that is broken. And if we are wounded, we need healing. Often healing begins with rest, with slowing down. The tension between action and faith is one we will explore in this lesson.

Encountering Jesus (15 minutes). The context of this story is that Jesus is on his way to the home of a religious leader, Jairus, to heal his daughter. Consider the possibility that Jesus sees in this woman not only as someone who needs to have her wounds bound but also as an opportunity for an object lesson for the Pharisees. Jairus is important and influential, while this woman is at the very bottom rung of the social ladder. Yet Jesus stops and makes Jairus wait while he talks with her. He could have healed her without having her step forward. In fact, the text says that she was healed as soon as she touched the hem of Jesus' clothes.

Her "unclean" status is the result of applying Leviticus 15:25-27 to her situation. Though some of these prohibitions in ancient Israel seem awkward to us, we must assume God had his reasons. Some stipulations in the law may have been designed as protection from disease, and some had spiritual overtones reminding people of their sin and need for redemption. Ceremonial uncleanness was a statement of one's need for reconciliation with God and with the community. A woman who had a continual discharge of blood would not have been able to marry, have a family or prepare meals for others. So the prohibition was designed to protect her, but it also isolated her, as none could touch her without being ceremonially (that is, religiously) unclean. Yet here, in full awareness of her condition, this woman touches Jesus.

We do not know for certain why he asks, "Who touched me?" but it is clear that Jesus, though limited by taking on flesh in a real body, knows the hearts of people. He predicts the future and sees deeply into people's minds. So it is likely that he is asking for information. It is more probable that, knowing her fear and her standing in the community as an "unclean" person, he had deeper purposes in mind:

1. to let her demonstrate her courage and testify to her healing
2. to teach Jairus that this "daughter" is as valuable to the kingdom as his daughter
3. to show others that faith, demonstrated in action, is what made this healing possible
4. to free her from her suffering and to demonstrate his power, even if he chooses not to heal all people

The woman is healed by her faith, not the touch itself. But the touching is the demonstration of her faith. Faith without works is dead, says James (see James 2:14-26). This demonstrates that Jesus' power to heal is accessible to all who believe by faith. Jesus heals often when people exercise faith. In some cases where there is little faith (Mark 9:21-24), he heals as well.

Joining the Conversation (20 minutes). Notice how Jesus addresses the woman. While all her life she has been called unclean and has been shamed, he calls her "daughter." This is the only time in the Bible that Jesus addresses a woman using this term. I imagine Jairus watching all this in disbelief and perhaps thinking, *Daughter? What about my daughter?* Jesus wants to bind our wounds—not just our physical wounds but the spiritual and emotional ones that may not be visible but are just as debilitating.

The disciples once again miss the point and, like us, miss the moment. Jesus is aware of the spiritual battles going on around him. We are often blind to them because we see with only our physical eyes.

Jesus heals not only the woman's physical wounds but also her scars of isolation, sadness, self-pity, loneliness. He heals deeply, calling the woman his treasured daughter, which suggests that salvation has come to her because of her faith in Jesus. So she is healed at many levels. She is healed socially: Jesus wants her to be restored to the community that has treated her as an outcast, probably because of the law. People could have touched her and shown compassion, but that would have meant ceremonial (not medical) uncleanness. She had been ignored and avoided.

Connecting Our Stories (20 minutes). You want the group to explore the connection between our faith and the changes that happen in our lives. However, it is very damaging to say to a person who needs healing, "You just need more faith." That's not what Jesus is implying in his words to this woman. Guide the group toward thinking about the connection between our faith, our actions and God's actions. There are not easy answers in this; it is quite mysterious. Resist the urge to tie up the loose ends.

Jesus has the conversation with this woman to complete her healing, to lift her up from the shame she had suffered, to allow her to give testimony when the society she lived in would have criticized and shamed her.

Keri Wyatt Kent writes about this woman's encounter with Jesus in her book *Breathe: Creating Space for God in a Hectic Life:*

> Jesus could have healed her quietly. He knew someone had touched him; I'm guessing he even knew who it was and everything she had been through. He could have let it go and saved the woman any embarrassment. Wouldn't that have been the gentlest thing? Why does he interrupt his interaction with Jairus to talk to this woman?
>
> Because he saw interruptions as an opportunity for ministry. He didn't see himself as too important to speak a word of loving affirmation to a person society saw as insignificant, undesirable, unclean. He was mindful

of the fact that his mission was to proclaim the good news that the kingdom of God is for everyone, not just people who appear to have it all together. He wanted to publicly affirm that to this woman. But he also wanted to teach the rest of the crowd, including Jairus, that truth as well.

Finding Our Way (10 minutes). God can heal directly but often uses the prayers and actions of people, especially for emotional healing. The key here is to see Jesus as a compassionate, powerful person. He is not obligated to heal and is no less loving when he does not heal immediately (as we see here and in the story of Lazarus). He has greater purposes. Sometimes it is our growth, which often can come only through suffering. Sometimes we lack faith. Sometimes it is simply that we need to bear the discipline or consequences of our poor decisions. What is clear is that Jesus is more concerned with inner, spiritual healing (salvation and growth) than with physical healing.

Praying Together (about 10 minutes). Sometimes God chooses not to heal our physical afflictions and instead chooses to heal our attitude. The apostle Paul, for example, suffered from some physical challenge—a thorn in his flesh, he called it. He prayed for it to be removed, but it wasn't. So he learned to be content in any circumstance (see 2 Corinthians 12:7-10 and Philippians 4:11-13).

SESSION 3.
JESUS CARRIES OUR BURDENS.
Luke 11:46; Matthew 9:35-38.

Gathering to Listen (about 10 minutes). Resist the urge to try to fix the problems or burdens people talk about. Each person can simply state briefly, in a few sentences, what burden they have. It may be related to their family life, their work or perhaps a conflict within the group. Don't try to solve the problem now. Simply name the burdens. You may want to have someone write them down. These specific burdens are among those Jesus wants to carry for us.

Unless it is absolutely necessary at this point in the meeting, guide the group gently away from lengthy discussion of burdens. The encounter with Jesus and with one another can be a means of ministering as members gain insight into their own stories and problems. There will be time at other points in the meeting for more discussion and specific prayer.

Encountering Jesus (15 minutes). If Jesus was fully human and fully God, then he is the one who gave the law to Moses in the first place. Before it got twisted by legalistic religion, the law reflected the heart of God and his desire to be in relationship with his people. God's law can be boiled down to two great commands: "love God, love each other." All the rest of the law hangs on these two simple—but difficult to practice—principles. It makes sense, then, that the Giver of such a law would be saddened and angered when people, especially religious leaders, twist the intent of the law, using it to manipulate and control others. As "experts" in the law, the Pharisees could circumvent the law or apply it to fit their social and political agenda. The Pharisees took legalism to an extreme and had enough political power to make people miserable. Jesus spoke out repeatedly against their abuses.

The Pharisees imposed a rules-and-regulations religion, creating hundreds of laws and commands beyond the biblical law and making it impossible for people to get near to the heart of God. As people struggled to observe all the detailed religious traditions of their leaders, they often felt burdened, wondering if they had successfully obeyed every little rule of the ceremonial and religious system. They felt guilty, inadequate, overwhelmed and insignificant when it came to knowing God.

The good news that Jesus brought was grace—a relationship with him. He was not interested in adding to the burdens people already experienced.

Joining the Conversation (20 minutes). Here we want to look honestly at two responses: Jesus' and our own. The world is not very kind to people who are helpless. We see that Jesus responds to such people with affection, compassion and truth. But how do we respond? With indifference, denial and condescension? Or are we ignorant of their plight because we are so busy? We easily become so consumed with our agendas and schedules that we ignore the plight of the helpless. But the Scripture is sobering: "If a man shuts his ears to the cry of the poor, he too will cry out and not be answered" (Proverbs 21:13).

Do not be afraid to probe the hearts of members. How do we all really respond? What will it take to change our hearts, to have the shepherd's heart of Jesus for lost sheep?

Connecting Our Stories (20 minutes). Be sensitive to the fact that the religious background of some group members may make them feel very much like the people of Jesus' day—burdened by legalism or judged and condemned. Without bashing any person or institution, gently challenge each group member to look at their background in light of what the Bible actually says. They may be angry or disillusioned with God because of what people have done or said to them. Urge them to seek the truth about God, and allow them time and space to process their feelings.

Sometimes people feel burdened because they are taking on things they were never meant to take on. It may be an issue of poor boundaries, where they are taking responsibility for other people's happiness or involved in a codependent relationship. Be aware of unhealthy patterns of relating that may be making a person feel burdened.

Use the list in question 8 to help people take a reality check on how they deal with their burdens. Ours is the most individualistic culture in history. Social observer Robert Bellah says such "rugged individualism" is a form of pride that keeps Americans unable to see their need for others. But we cannot do life alone. We need God and others to help us find the way.

Finding Our Way (10 minutes). Jesus uses the metaphor of workers and a harvest to point out that God often accomplishes his purposes through people. While this verse is often cited to motivate evangelism, it's possible that Jesus is talking about not just saving souls but also bearing one another's burdens. Part of how Jesus bears our burdens is to bring people into our lives to share those burdens. Challenge group members to determine how, specifically, they can help bear the burdens of others. This does not mean taking care of everyone but rather listening to God and looking at your life experiences to see where you might encourage or help someone else.

The passages in Matthew and Galatians are there for added reinforcement. As you briefly read these texts, people will see again God's approach to burden lifting. We come to Jesus and we run to others. Though we each have a responsibility to carry our own load (our own backpack), we are to help carry the difficult and wearying burdens (the huge boulders) of one another.

Praying Together (about 10 minutes). Here's an exercise that may be helpful. Get some smooth rocks (sometimes you can find these at craft stores or nurseries), about the size you can hold in your hand easily—not too small. Using fine-point permanent markers, let each group member write a word or two on a rock that describes their burden. For example, someone overwhelmed by caring for an aging parent might write "Mom's health" on their rock. Allow the group to spend some time thinking about their burdens and writing a word or short phrase on their rocks. Sit in a circle. Then ask group members to describe what is written on their rock, in as much detail as they feel is appropriate.

Then pray for each, and have members place the rocks on the floor in the middle of the circle to symbolize letting go of the burden and letting Jesus carry it. Then, as a community, pile the rocks together to build an altar. In the Old Testament, when God rescued his people or showed up in a powerful way, or when they were beseeching God to do just that, they would build an altar of rocks. A time of reflection or worship may follow, or silent prayer. As you close, allow each member to take their rock with them as a reminder of God's strength and the group's commitment to support one another.

SESSION 4.
JESUS BREAKS OUR CHAINS.
Luke 13:10-17.

Gathering to Listen (about 10 minutes). Encourage the group to think metaphorically. How are group members held captive; how are they blind, poor, oppressed?

Encountering Jesus (15 minutes). Like this woman, many of us are prisoners of pain. The woman was bent over, her back was bowed. She was physically crippled. Some people in your group may be suffering physical pain, others emotional pain.

Spend some time just painting the scene: Jesus is teaching but stops when he notices the woman. Though not translated fully in the NIV, the front part of verse 11 can be translated "and look, a woman . . ." as if Jesus is drawing particular public attention to her. It is as though he is saying, "Look, everyone! Here is a crippled woman in desperate need of healing. And we all know she has come to the right place—a house of worship on the sabbath day!"

He interrupts his sermon to bring her up in front of the crowd. Perhaps she is embarrassed by the attention. As she looks out at the crowd, she sees the Pharisees and synagogue ruler frowning and whispering among themselves. She may feel frightened. But she is courageous. When she is healed, she does not slink away. She stands up straight for the first time in eighteen years, perhaps lifting her hands and singing or shouting to God. Imagine the electricity in the air—the amazement of the crowd, the anger of the Pharisees.

Just as in Luke 6, where Jesus heals a man with a withered hand on the sabbath in a synagogue, members of the religious elite are furious. They want more than anything to catch Jesus breaking the law so they can accuse and arrest him. And they are interested in sabbath keeping more as a ritual than as an expression of devotion toward God. They are blind and ignorant of the work of God that changes lives.

As Jesus becomes more popular as a teacher and leader, the Pharisees are increasingly jealous and worried that he will take over. The irony is, they are using the very system that "chains" them—the legalism that Jesus says is not the way to God—as a way to try to trap him. They seek to ensnare him with the letter of the law, but he counters their attack by reminding them that it is the spirit of the law that matters. They are confounded by his wisdom and angry that he will not join them in their legalistic chains. He offers them freedom, but they refuse it.

The word *demon* is not used here, but a spirit is afflicting the woman. Jesus touches her in this case (nowhere else do we read of him touching demon-possessed people). So this may not be a possession as much as an affliction, behind which is the power of sin and Satan (see 13:16). Jesus is the one who recognizes the spiritual oppression she is under as a result of the activity of the evil one.

Joining the Conversation (20 minutes). Help the group understand that people with chronic illness or disability may experience a range of emotions, from guilt to anger to helplessness. They may be angry at God, upset at others who cannot understand their condition, or ashamed of themselves.

Use the list in question 5 simply as a way of helping people identify with the characters in the story, to take their point of view as they encounter Jesus.

- The crippled woman may feel ashamed but also hopeful.
- The spirit that keeps her bound would be angry and intimidated by Jesus.
- The synagogue ruler would be offended and fear losing control of the situation.
- The people who are watching are elated and thrilled at God's power.
- Other religious leaders are humiliated and feel rage toward Jesus.
- Satan feels defeated.

Now let people describe how they think they would respond. Avoid trite answers. Would people really be like Jesus or like the crowd that was delighted? Would some feel disappointed because Jesus heals this woman but has not healed them?

Connecting Our Stories (20 minutes). The theme of freedom is woven throughout Jesus' ministry. The Pharisees wanted to keep people oppressed to make themselves look good and to build up their power.

Some people in your group may have been, or may still be, in bondage to an addiction of some sort; it may be drugs or alcohol, or perhaps something more socially acceptable, like shopping or people pleasing.

Just as the Pharisees turned the wisdom of God's law into an oppressive set of rules, some people today have turned Jesus' teaching into the bondage of legalism. Guide the group toward exploring what it really means to be "set free."

Finding Our Way (10 minutes). Ask the group to think about ways that they can set each other free: perhaps by loving each other, by being more generous with encouragement than criticism, by reminding each other of the truth of grace. This does not mean that we ignore sinful patterns in others in our community but that we lovingly call forth the best in the people around us.

It may be good to read Galatians 5:1-2 to the group as a reminder. If some need more than this, encourage them to read Galatians 5 in their quiet time over the next few days, making note of the differences between a life of freedom and a life steeped in legalistic or moralistic working to please God. Paul makes the case for our freedom in Christ.

Praying Together (about 10 minutes). Before prayer you may want to read John 8:31-36 and talk briefly about what it means to be set free by Jesus. He frees us from sin and guilt when we enter into relationship with him. The comments in John 8:31 and following are directed toward people who believed in him but were still trying to hang on to their old way of life.

SESSION 5.
JESUS COVERS OUR SHAME.
John 8:1-11.

Gathering to Listen (about 10 minutes). Shame is self-defeating. It is different from guilt that results from sinning. Guilt says, "I have done something bad." Shame says, "I am a bad person."

When we label people, we are making character judgments and assigning value to another. Labels can become our identity or can influence how we view ourselves. The boy whose father beats him, believing the boy is "good for nothing," will likely become an angry boy. As he grows, he seeks to prove he is somebody and is not weak, so he bullies others. Others in such a situation may shrink back and withdraw from the world, believing they are truly no good to anyone. Shame is indeed a powerful emotion.

Encountering Jesus (15 minutes). It should be noted that this section of the Bible, John 7:53—8:11, does not appear in many of the earliest surviving manuscripts of the Gospel of John. Some scholars have thus argued that though this may be a true story, it should not be included at this point in the Gospel of John and that it does not fit with the flow of the book. Though its origins and authenticity may be questioned, the story's concepts and the response of Jesus it recounts are in keeping with his character as revealed in other Scriptures. So, if this was not an actual event, it at least serves as a parable. Jesus' actions as portrayed here are consistent with other aspects of his teachings and miracles.

Jesus' teaching unravels the tightly held convictions of the Pharisees. Obviously, this makes them uncomfortable. It's likely that they have somehow set this woman up to get caught in the bed of a man who is not her husband. Or they simply know she has been in such a situation and cannot refute their accusations. Given that it is early in the morning, she may have been dragged to the temple half naked or wrapped in a bed sheet.

Before she is brought to Jesus, she has been paraded through the streets of the city, exposing her shame and causing great humiliation. It appears from the account that she does not even speak or seek to challenge her accusers.

The Pharisees are basing their actions on Leviticus 20:10: "If a man commits adultery with another man's wife—with the wife of his neighbor—both the adulterer and the adulteress must be put to death." However, they have not brought the man with them. That is why some interpreters of this text believe that the woman was framed, or that she had committed the act in the past and was an easy target, or that she was a prostitute. If she was framed, it was likely that the man had been paid to comply with the Pharisees and was promised immunity from any accusation. In any case, they are taking advantage of a woman who cannot defend herself against her accusers.

The legalistic Pharisees and teachers hope to catch Jesus denying or even defying the law of Moses. But he is keenly aware of their trickery. He writes in the sand. His actions create tension, while the Pharisees wonder whether he will break or uphold the law. If he upholds the letter of the law, then he must condone stoning the woman, and certainly they will blame Jesus for the stoning. But if he exonerates her, he defies the law, and the Jews have religious grounds to accuse him.

As he often does, Jesus turns the situation to his advantage and exposes the true hearts of people around him. (Mark 11:30-33 is another instance in which Jesus turns the tables on those who seek to trap and accuse him.)

Joining the Conversation (20 minutes). The important thing here is the relationship of accusation to judgment and condemnation. These leaders first accuse the woman of breaking the law of Moses. They point the finger. They come with a group of people, because any accusation had to be supported by two or three witnesses. Catching the woman in the act would have required the cooperation of a few people to make the accusation stick. They could have taken her to a priest or a religious ruler, but they want to trap Jesus.

To pass judgment (negatively) is to decide the motives and character of a person before knowing the facts. These religious zealots have made themselves judge and jury, seeking to have the woman punished for her sin or trap Jesus—or both.

Once judgment has been passed, condemnation seals her fate. She is condemned to die. The sentence is about to be carried out. These men have accused, judged and condemned the woman without any real process. Wanting the sentence to be carried out immediately, they seek to incite the crowd of onlookers into a frenzy. But Jesus will have none of this; he slows things down and presses people to examine not only the law written on stone tablets but the law written on their hearts.

Jesus' disciples are sometimes baffled by his parables or the things he did. This is one of those times. Yet, as Card points out, his silence is more effective than a lecture at this point. Card points out that in Jesus' silence, God speaks to the hearts of the accusing mob. Guide the group toward discussing how God speaks in silence.

Connecting Our Stories (20 minutes). When we are caught doing something we know is wrong, there is regret and shame. Often we try to rationalize and say we didn't know better or were set up. But the truth is, we feel shame. If we didn't, we wouldn't feel the need to rationalize or make excuses. (This woman either has no chance of defending herself or truly is guilty for the crime she is accused of.)

If we have trusted Christ as our forgiver and seek to follow him as master and leader of our life, we have received grace. This may be an appropriate place for you to briefly recount your own testimony. Be simple and direct, avoid using Christian jargon that seekers in the group may not understand. Like this woman, we all have sinned, and we stand accused by the evil one, but Jesus offers us grace and forgiveness, not condemnation.

Finding Our Way (10 minutes). The point of this study is not that Jesus winks at our sin or ignores it but that he offers us a second chance and calls us to change. When we can admit our shortcomings, we can begin to seek a new way of life, one that is free from shame and guilt.

Challenge the group to get as specific as possible about ways that they can offer grace to each other and to other people that they encounter in daily life.

Praying Together (about 10 minutes). You may want to talk about what it means to be "in Christ Jesus" and how that relationship with Jesus brings us the freedom Paul writes about in Romans 8:1. Part of accepting Christ's covering of our shame is being willing to acknowledge our sin against God (true guilt or sorrow) and to let go of shame (*I will always be a bad person*) by entering into a relationship with him. Jesus gives us a new identity. Jesus carried our shame, dying a shameful death on the cross. People were stripped naked when they were crucified, a public humiliation for all and especially shameful to a Jew. Christ's death mysteriously took the shame of all humankind and placed it upon himself.

As you pray, together or in subgroups, look for opportunities to affirm the standing believers have in Christ, and be aware of those who are still trying to understand this concept as they search for resolution of their own feelings of shame and guilt.

SESSION 6.
JESUS RESTORES OUR COMMUNITY.
John 17:6-26.

Gathering to Listen (about 10 minutes). When we dwell in unity, God blesses us abundantly. But unity requires us to be loving and forgiving.

Encountering Jesus (15 minutes). Jesus' oneness with the Father is the foundation for his prayer. He wants us to live in the same kind of relationship he has with the heavenly Father and, by implication, the Holy Spirit. Such a relationship is impossible within our community unless we are willing to allow Christ to guide us. Jesus is interceding for us, praying that we will take action to act as one in his name.

Some of the characteristics of his relationship with his disciples are deep connection, obedience, receptivity to God's Word and belief. These constitute the foundation for sharing life in Christ.

In verses 13-19 the new community—the unified group of believers—should exhibit certain characteristics, according to Jesus' request:

- experience his joy (verse 13)
- receive and grow from the truth of his Word (verses 14, 17)
- be protected from division (verse 15)
- grow in holiness (verse 17)
- have a mission to reach others (verse 18)

In addition, in verses 24-26 Jesus prays that the love and glory he shares with the Father would be ours as well.

Joining the Conversation (20 minutes). Jesus prays for protection from the evil one in this prayer (see verses 11, 15) and in what we commonly call the Lord's Prayer (Matthew 6:9-13). Protection from what—disease, illness, persecution? No. Given the context of the prayer in John 17 and what we know of the strategy of the evil one (his desire to divide and destroy), Jesus is praying for protection from division. After all, the power of the gospel message is at stake (verses 21-23, "that the world may know").

Those who did not grow up in the church may not be aware of how in recent decades walls between denominations have fallen, at least in the United States. Only a couple of generations ago, Baptists, Presbyterians, Pentecostals, Catholics, Lutherans and the like each thought the others were misguided and blind.

Today there is much less animosity between Protestant denominations, and even between Protestants and Catholics. However, in other parts of the world there is anything but unity between Protestants and Catholics (in Ireland, for example).

Unity does not mean that we agree that all roads lead to God or that everyone is right—that's a logical impossibility. Help the group grapple with what unity really does mean. Which issues are essential? Which ones are less important areas where we can "agree to disagree"?

Connecting Our Stories (20 minutes). Jesus' followers today still have a long way to go to reach the level of oneness that he experienced with the Father. The fact that many conflicts around the globe stem from religious differences can be a bit overwhelming, and we may feel as if there is nothing we can do to address such a thorny problem.

It may be impossible to achieve world peace, but we can make peace with our neighbors. We can love the people in our church, in our small group, in our neighborhood. We can join Jesus in his prayer for unity and then move into the world to put into action the vision in our heart. It is the only way that the oneness Jesus described will ever happen.

Living in complete unity is a desired goal for which lovers of Jesus should work and pray. It begins with individuals we know. To live in unity means agreeing to a common cause, expressing love and forgiveness when we are wronged, engaging in debate without condemning one another, serving one another and praying for each other—even our enemies.

As you look at Ephesians 4, remind members of what those who follow Jesus have in common: one Lord, a common faith, an identity together in Christ. We are one community through the cross and share one Spirit. This is the foundation of our unity. These great truths should unite us, even as we have disagreements on other areas of biblical teaching and theology.

The world will take notice of Christian unity created in love. Not all will choose to follow Christ as a result, but the world will have to admit that our oneness is unique and powerful.

Finding Our Way (10 minutes). Building unity does not mean avoiding conflict. Often unity requires that we lovingly confront. Often it means that we must forgive even if it is difficult, even if we have been wronged. Again, Ephesians 4 is helpful, especially verses 25-32. Guide participants toward thinking not about what other people or institutions should do but about what step they can take toward building the unity that Christ calls us to.

Praying Together (about 10 minutes). Sometimes it is hard to admit that there are walls of division. And even when we admit they exist, it's easy to blame them on other people. You may want to pray the words of Ephesians 2:14, along these lines: "Lord Jesus, please be our peace and break down the dividing walls of hostility." Encourage group members to take responsibility for their part in any conflict or disunity they are experiencing. Commit yourselves together to be a force in the world of not just truth but love as well, expressed in oneness.

Also available from InterVarsity Press and Willow Creek Resources

BIBLE 101. *Where truth meets life.*
Bill Donahue, series editor

The Bible 101 series is designed for those who want to know how to study God's Word, understand it clearly and apply it to their lives in a way that produces personal transformation. Geared especially for groups, the series can also profitably be used for individual study. Each guide has five sessions that overview essential information and teach new study skills. The sixth session brings the skills together in a way that relates them to daily life.

FOUNDATIONS: *How We Got Our Bible*
Bill Donahue

TIMES & PLACES: *Picturing the Events of the Bible*
Michael Redding

COVER TO COVER: *Getting the Bible's Big Picture*
Gerry Mathisen

STUDY METHODS: *Experiencing the Power of God's Word*
Kathy Dice

INTERPRETATION: *Discovering the Bible for Yourself*
Judson Poling

PARABLES & PROPHECY: *Unlocking the Bible's Mysteries*
Bill Donahue

GREAT THEMES: *Understanding the Bible's Core Doctrines*
Michael Redding

PERSONAL DEVOTION: *Taking God's Word to Heart*
Kathy Dice